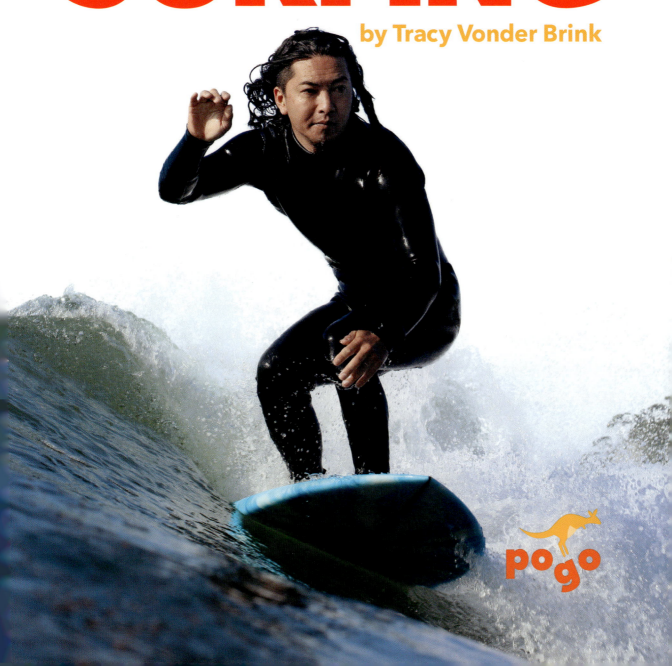

EXTREME SPORTS
SURFING

by Tracy Vonder Brink

Ideas for Parents and Teachers

Pogo Books let children practice reading informational text while introducing them to nonfiction features such as headings, labels, sidebars, maps, and diagrams, as well as a table of contents, glossary, and index.

Carefully leveled text with a strong photo match offers early fluent readers the support they need to succeed.

Before Reading

- "Walk" through the book and point out the various nonfiction features. Ask the student what purpose each feature serves.
- Look at the glossary together. Read and discuss the words.

Read the Book

- Have the child read the book independently.
- Invite them to list questions that arise from reading.

After Reading

- Discuss the child's questions. Talk about how they might find answers to those questions.
- Prompt the child to think more. Ask: Would you like to surf? Why or why not?

Pogo Books are published by Jump!
5357 Penn Avenue South
Minneapolis, MN 55419
www.jumplibrary.com

Copyright © 2025 Jump!
International copyright reserved in all countries. No part of this book may be reproduced in any form without written permission from the publisher.

Library of Congress Cataloging-in-Publication Data

Names: Vonder Brink, Tracy, author.
Title: Surfing / by Tracy Vonder Brink.
Description: Minneapolis, MN: Jump!, Inc., 2025.
Series: Extreme sports | Includes index.
Audience: Ages 7-10
Identifiers: LCCN 2024037510 (print)
LCCN 2024037511 (ebook)
ISBN 9798892136488 (hardcover)
ISBN 9798892136495 (paperback)
ISBN 9798892136501 (ebook)
Subjects: LCSH: Surfing—Juvenile literature.
Sports science—Juvenile literature.
Classification: LCC GV839.55 .V66 2025 (print)
LCC GV839.55 (ebook)
DDC 797.3/2—dc23/eng/20240919
LC record available at https://lccn.loc.gov/2024037510
LC ebook record available at https://lccn.loc.gov/2024037511

Editor: Alyssa Sorenson
Designer: Molly Ballanger

Photo Credits: Don White/iStock, cover; Dane Gillett/Shutterstock, 1, 23; Delbars/Shutterstock, 3; wavebreakmedia/Shutterstock, 4; Dane Gillett/iStock, 5; Nuture/iStock, 6-7; Cavan Images/SuperStock, 8; AleksandarNakic/iStock, 9; SOMA surf-therapy/Shutterstock, 10-11; homydesign/iStock, 12-13; Longjourneys/Shutterstock, 14; Neil Bradfield/Shutterstock, 15; ChrisVanLennepPhoto/Shutterstock, 16-17; trubavin/Shutterstock, 18-19; Koji Hirano/Getty, 20-21.

Printed in the United States of America at Corporate Graphics in North Mankato, Minnesota.

TABLE OF CONTENTS

CHAPTER 1
Riding Waves 4

CHAPTER 2
Surfing Basics 8

CHAPTER 3
Surfing Tricks 14

ACTIVITIES & TOOLS
Try This! 22
Glossary 23
Index 24
To Learn More 24

CHAPTER 1
RIDING WAVES

A surfer lies belly-down on their surfboard. They use their arms to paddle into the ocean.

They stop and wait. They look for the right wave. It should have smooth water. Why? Smooth water makes for an easier ride. The wave must also move fast enough to carry the surfer.

CHAPTER 1   5

CHAPTER 1

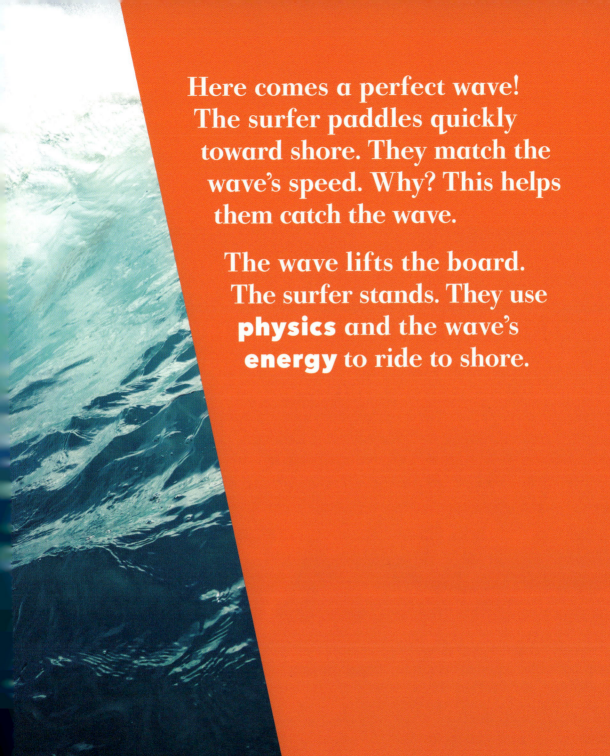

Here comes a perfect wave! The surfer paddles quickly toward shore. They match the wave's speed. Why? This helps them catch the wave.

The wave lifts the board. The surfer stands. They use **physics** and the wave's **energy** to ride to shore.

CHAPTER 1   7

CHAPTER 2
SURFING BASICS

Physics helps a surfer move forward. It starts when they paddle into the water. Every action has an equal and opposite reaction. When a surfer pushes against the water, the water pushes back. This moves the board forward.

Gravity pulls a surfboard down. But buoyancy pushes it up. These forces balance each other. The surfboard floats.

When a surfer stands up, they bend their knees. Why? This keeps their **center of gravity** low. It helps them balance and stay on the board.

DID YOU KNOW?

Surfers put sticky wax on their boards. Why? It creates **friction** under their feet. This keeps them from slipping off the board.

 CHAPTER 2

Surfers **shift** their weight to turn. For example, to turn left, the surfer moves their weight to their back foot. Then they push down with the left side of their foot. This makes the board turn to the left.

CHAPTER 2

TAKE A LOOK!

How does a surfer catch a wave? Take a look!

❶ ❷ ❸ ❹

SHORE

❶ Wind creates a wave.

❷ The surfer paddles toward shore. The wave lifts the board.

❸ The surfer stands up. Gravity pulls them down.

❹ The surfer turns their board. They ride along the wave's side as the wave pushes them to shore.

CHAPTER 3
SURFING TRICKS

A wave rolls in. Its energy slows as it reaches shore. This makes the wave fall forward. Some falling waves have a space inside. This space is called a tube.

tube

mist

How do you know if a tube will form? The wave sprays **mist** as it falls. The mist tells surfers to get ready to ride.

CHAPTER 3 15

The wave carries the surfer inside the tube. They touch the wall. Why? Dragging their hand creates friction. This slows them down. They ride inside the tube longer.

CHAPTER 3

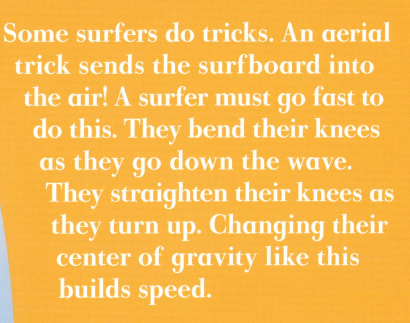

Some surfers do tricks. An aerial trick sends the surfboard into the air! A surfer must go fast to do this. They bend their knees as they go down the wave. They straighten their knees as they turn up. Changing their center of gravity like this builds speed.

The board heads to the top of the wave. The surfer kicks their back foot down. This sends the board into the air!

DID YOU KNOW?

A surfer's ride is short. Many only last 10 to 20 seconds!

CHAPTER 3

Hawaii's Banzai Pipeline has some of the world's biggest and fastest waves. Surfers **compete** at events in Hawaii and around the world. Understanding science helps them win!

> ### DID YOU KNOW?
>
> Some waves are huge! The biggest wave ever surfed was in Portugal in 2024. It was almost 94 feet (29 meters) tall! That is almost as high as a 10-story building.

ACTIVITIES & TOOLS

TRY THIS!

MAKE IT FLOAT

Buoyancy helps a surfboard float. Explore how it works with this fun activity!

What You Need:
- modeling clay
- rolling pin
- large bowl of water

❶ Make a ball out of the clay. Make it about twice the size of a marble.

❷ Place the clay ball in the bowl of water. What happens?

❸ Take the clay ball out of the water. Set it on a flat surface. Use the rolling pin to roll it out thin.

❹ Place the flattened clay in the water. What happens?

❺ Why do you think one sank and one floated? How is the flattened piece of clay like a surfboard?

GLOSSARY

buoyancy: The upward force on an object floating in liquid.

center of gravity: The point on an object at which half of its weight is on one side and half is on the other.

compete: To try to win a contest.

energy: The ability to do work.

forces: Things that cause objects to move or change their speed or direction.

friction: The force that slows down objects when they rub against each other.

gravity: The force that pulls things toward the center of Earth and keeps them from floating away.

mist: A cloud of tiny water droplets that hangs in the air.

physics: The science that deals with matter, energy, and their interactions.

shift: To move from one position to another.

ACTIVITIES & TOOLS 23

INDEX

balance 9, 10
Banzai Pipeline 20
buoyancy 9
center of gravity 10, 19
compete 20
energy 7, 14
floats 9
friction 10, 16
gravity 9, 13, 19
mist 15

paddle 4, 7, 8, 13
physics 7, 8
shore 7, 13, 14
speed 7, 19
surfboard 4, 7, 8, 9, 10, 12, 13, 19
tricks 19
tube 14, 15, 16
turn 12, 13, 19
wave 5, 7, 13, 14, 15, 16, 19, 20
wax 10

TO LEARN MORE

Finding more information is as easy as 1, 2, 3.
❶ Go to www.factsurfer.com
❷ Enter "surfing" into the search box.
❸ Choose your book to see a list of websites.

ACTIVITIES & TOOLS